Davy Crockett
Daniel Boone

Pendulum Press, Inc.
West Haven, Connecticut

ISBN 0-88301-424-6 Complete Set
    0-88301-351-7 Paperback
    0-88301-363-0 Hardcover

Library of Congress Catalog Card Number 79-83612

Published by
Pendulum Press, Inc.
An Academic Industries, Inc. Company
The Academic Building
Saw Mill Road
West Haven, Connecticut 06516

Printed in the United States of America

To the teacher

Every parent and teacher knows that youngsters often model their lives after those of people they admire. Sometimes this works well, as in the case of a boy named Erich Weiss. Reading the biography of the French magician Houdin, Erich was so fascinated that he changed his name and eventually became the great Houdini, the world-famous escape artist. But children don't always choose worthwhile models; we shudder to think they might imitate one or another of the unsavory characters they see on TV. It is precisely to counterbalance this mix of dubious screen heroes that Pendulum presents its illustrated biography series.

Like the Pendulum illustrated classics series that preceded them, these biographies are the result of painstaking research and writing. The artwork throughout is first-quality illustration; the type, an easy-to-read sans-serif style. Tested with both the Dale-Chall List and the Fry Readability Scale, each book is edited to an intermediate-grade vocabulary level. Yet the material is suitable for practically everyone regardless of age or reading prowess.

How you, the teacher, will use this series is of great interest to us. We have tried to provide you with a varied, interesting, and self-motivating teaching tool. We think your students will like our selection of famous people and the format we used to illustrate their lives. If you or they have any questions, suggestions, or comments on the series, we would like to hear them. As always, Pendulum wants to provide your students with the best materials possible.

The editors

Davy Crockett

Written by
NAUNERLE C. FARR

Illustrated by
FRED CARRILLO

a
VINCENT FAGO
production

Contents

At the Alamo,* U. S. forces fought to free Texas from Mexico. Among the soldiers was Davy Crockett, a hero who vowed** to die rather than give up the fort. This is his story.

*a large fort in Texas that was attacked by the Mexicans during the Mexican-American War
**promised, swore

In 1786, fifty years before the battle at the Alamo, a band of Indians attacked a cabin* in Tennessee.

The owner, David Crockett, and some of his family were killed.

A short time later, only a few miles away, a ninth child was born to his son, John Crockett.

A boy! I want to name him David, after my father.

Yes, and we'll call him Davy.

Young Davy learned early how to handle a gun.

You're eight years old, son. Think you can go hunting by yourself?

Yes, sir!

*a small house, often made of logs

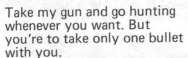

Take my gun and go hunting whenever you want. But you're to take only one bullet with you.

Any time you miss your shot, you'll go to bed without supper!

Y-yes, sir!

Davy soon became the best shot in a country full of sharpshooters.* He grew up. He liked dances. At one he met a girl named Polly Finlay.

There's a shooting match coming up, Polly. If I could win the prize, I'd have a question to ask you.

I'll be waiting, Davy . . . and cheering for you!

More than eighty men entered the contest. The first prize was a cow.

Each man has one shot from fifty yards away. The best shooters will try again from seventy-five, and so on.

*people who can shoot very well

Davy used his father's gun called "Old Betsy." He reached the last test, at one hundred yards.

I can hit that target* with one eye shut. Come on, Old Betsy!

A bull's-eye! The winner . . . young Davy Crockett!

Davy sold his cow for five gold dollars. Then he went to Polly's house.

I'd like mighty well to change your name from Polly Finlay to Mrs. David Crockett.

And I'd like that, too!

Two weeks later they were married, and moved to their new home.

It's lovely, Davy . . . our own home!

Just as long as I pay the twenty-five cents a month rent!

*something that is shot at

After a year they had a baby boy.

I want my children to grow up in a new country! There's fine land and great hunting in south Tennessee!

How far away is it? How would we get there?

A week's travel by boat would do it. We wouldn't have to take much with us.

The next spring, Polly agreed to move, even though by then there were two babies. Davy and Polly went to look for a boat to take them south.

Hey, Captain . . . do you have room for us?

Sure have! Come right aboard!

The boat floated at last into the big Tennessee River. Davy's family slept in bunks on top of the cabin. Other passengers came and left again.

Look at that deer! This is great country for hunting!

Finally they reached the end of the boat trip.

Where do we go now?

There's a trail over the mountains that leads to a river valley.

It was fine weather. They camped along the trail.

Here's dinner! Is the pot ready? I've never seen so much game!*

In a few days they found a good place to settle. Davy built a small cabin.

This is a good cabin, Davy.

I'll soon cover that dirt floor with bear skins!

He was right. During the next year, Davy killed 105 bears.

All right, Growler, Deathmaul, Grim, Holdfast!** Steady . . .

Soon people everywhere knew not only Davy's name, but the names of his dogs too.

*animals to hunt, such as deer, elk, bears, and wild turkeys
**the names of Davy's dogs

Word of them spread all over Tennessee.

That young Davy Crockett's killed enough bears to feed every person in the county! And enough raccoons* to make a cap for every man and boy!

But the year was 1812. There was other more important news.

We're at war with England again. And the English** are trying to get the Indians to fight against us.

At Fort Mims in Alabama, the Indians wiped out a whole town. Maybe the country can use another sharpshooter.

Oh, Davy! Don't go to war!

My grandfather fought the English—father, too. Now it's my turn. It won't be for long, Polly.

So Davy went off with his gun, leaving his dogs behind. He headed for a camp where he knew men were gathering. Among them was Colonel John Coffee.

This is a good place for a camp—but where's the army?

It's on the way. And General Andrew Jackson's leading it!

*small, gray animals with bushy, ringed tails; the fur and tails were used to make hats
**people from England

Trouble is, the food has been held up somewhere. There's nothing to eat but a little flour, salt, and molasses.*

No meat? I can get us some. There are signs of bears around here.

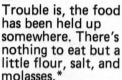

I've heard you are the best bear hunter in Tennessee . . . .

That's a lie! I'm the best bear hunter on earth!

Davy took a few men and left camp. Soon General Jackson arrived with the army.

I've brought plenty of guns and powder, but not much food.

That's too bad, because we have no food here!

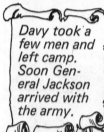

Just then they heard a loud noise and saw a strange parade coming toward them.

It's Davy Crockett, the Tennessee bear hunter!

And a good 500 pounds of bear! The men won't go to bed hungry.

*a thick, dark, sweet syrup

Soon General Jackson had 1,500 men to fight the Indians. But he was worried.

Every day there are more reports of Indian attacks. But my men have never been in a battle. They need training!

We can wait no longer. How many good fighting men could you pick out of this bunch?

Would fifty help?

Coffee was put in charge of the fifty men, with Major Russell and Davy Crockett under him. They were to find the Indians.

For a month they tracked Indian raiding parties* with no luck. Then . . .

He says there's an Indian camp about a day's ride away. He'll guide us.

Saddle your horses!

At dawn the next day, Coffee and his men attacked. Bullets and arrows flew through the air.

In ten minutes the battle was over. Thirty-eight Indian braves** were dead. The rest ran into the woods, leaving only women and children behind.

*small groups of Indians who attacked towns and villages
**Indian warriors

Davy was the only white man who knew the Indians' language.

The women think they will be killed.

Tell them to get their things. We'll take them to the army camp where they'll be safe.

Back at the main army camp there was a new problem.

This man says 200 friendly Indians and several white families are at Fort Talladega. They are being attacked by 1,100 Creeks.*

The Creeks had said that unless those in the fort joined them against the whites, they would kill them all. Jackson and his army started to move.

He sent Davy and Russell ahead to look things over.

The Creeks can take that fort any time they try!

They're telling the Indians inside the fort to come out by tomorrow!

We've got to help those poor Indians inside the fort. They're on our side! I'll ride back and find General Jackson!

Davy rode fast through the woods.

If the Creeks have a scout** posted, they'll see me for sure.

*a group or tribe of Indians that lived in Alabama, Georgia, and Florida
**someone who keeps watch or makes a search

He found Jackson's camp six miles back. Quickly, Jackson told 500 men to follow Crockett. They reached the fort just after sunrise.

The Creeks know we're here. Divide your men and circle the fort. I'll attack from behind.

Bravely Russell and his men moved forward. The Creeks were waiting for them in thick bushes. They rushed out to attack.

Then Crockett and his men attacked from behind. When the Creeks ran, they met American guns shooting from the other side of the fort.

The battle was soon over. Seventeen white men had died. Four hundred and thirty Creeks had been killed, but 800 had escaped.

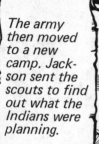

The army then moved to a new camp. Jackson sent the scouts to find out what the Indians were planning.

A strong group of Indians is gathered on the Tallapoosa River, close to the ford.*

That's where they expect us to cross. I'll bet a thousand Indians are waiting there to ambush** us!

We'll cross five miles down the river. It's harder, but we'll surprise them and attack from the other side.

At first, everything went as planned. The main army crossed the river. The cannons crossed. Then the scouts followed.

Major, the Indians! They're attacking from behind us!

The Indians had learned of Jackson's plan. They made a surprise attack from the rear, catching the scouts in midstream.

*a shallow place in a river where men, horses, and wagons can cross
**take by surprise

Jackson's men had never been in battle before. Instead of firing at the Indians, they ran for the woods. Colonel Carroll shouted after them.

Come back!

Charging through the water, the scouts forced their way ashore and into hand-to-hand combat* with the Indians.

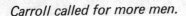

Carroll called for more men.

General Jackson himself came back to help fire the cannon.

Steady, now! Aim the cannon.

Aim well, men!

*fighting

The cannon fire was too much for the Indians. They ran back into the woods.

The Tallapoosa River Battle was nearly the end of the war with the Creeks. Soon they signed a peace treaty.*

But Davy did not like the treaty.

I've killed many an Indian, but now I'm sorry. This treaty is not fair to the Indians!

I'm an Army man, Davy. I do what I'm told.

I'm a hunter and a fighter, but I guess I'm no Army man. I'll be glad to get out of it.

From then on, Davy was a friend of the Indians.

He left the army and went home. The children were well, but not his Polly.

I'll be well in no time, now that you're home, Davy!

Instead, Polly soon died. Sadly, Davy buried her, and marked her grave with a large rock.

*an agreement made by two or more groups to stop a war they are fighting

Elizabeth Patton, whose husband had been killed in the war, lived nearby with her two children. She was lonely. Davy was lonely without Polly, too.

After a while, Davy asked Elizabeth to marry him.

Why don't we get together and make one big, happy family?

That's fine, Davy.

Then the Crocketts moved farther west. Their new neighbors were glad to see them.

We'd be proud to have such a well-known scout around here, Colonel Crockett!

Soon they elected Colonel Crockett a judge.*

A judge needs to read law. I'll have to work on it.

Meanwhile, Davy built the first grist mill** in the neighborhood.

Mighty handy to get my corn and wheat ground so close to home.

It sure is. I'm glad to help.

*someone who decides questions brought before a court
**a building where grain is ground into flour

Not long after this, Davy was elected* to the state government. When he came home he found that a flood had washed away his mill.

Don't worry, dear. We'll sell everything and move west.

That's the kind of talk I like! Maybe we can find a place where the hunting's still good!

In 1822, the Crocketts settled in a wild place near the Tennessee River.

Greatest country I ever saw! There are bears, deer, raccoons . . . and the nearest neighbor's eight miles away!

Will you teach us to hunt, Pa?

I'll teach you all I know about it, son!

For the next few years, Davy often took his sons with him into the woods.

*chosen by a vote

The Tennessee bear hunter was becoming known all over the country. Strangers often stopped to hear his stories.

I've heard that you hunt alligators, too, Mr. Crockett.

Well, yes. As a matter of fact, I like to tame them. I'd rather ride on a gator than in a canoe —faster ride, less work!

Two of the strangers had a different question.

Crockett, will you run for congressman* from Tennessee?

Not now. I've just started a business. But some other time I might say yes.

Davy's business was making and selling staves.** He had a group of men cutting down trees and making the staves. Another group was building flat boats.

I'll float 30,000 staves down the Mississippi on these two boats. Then we'll sell them in New Orleans.

Davy hired a man named Captain Whale to pilot the boats.

Welcome, Captain! I hear you're one of the best pilots on these rivers.

That's true, Mr. Crockett —if I do say so!

*a person who serves in one of the houses of the U.S. government
**narrow pieces of wood that are wired together to make barrels

But on the big Mississippi, Captain Whale did not seem to know what to do.

Were you ever a pilot on *this* river?

Well, I . . . I was an assistant* pilot once!

Davy had the men tie both boats together. Night came.

When are we going to tie up for the night?

Well . . . uh . . . pretty soon.

But Whale did not know how to bring a boat to shore! And on a bad part of the river known as Devil's Elbow, they crashed into an island.

Every man for himself!

*helper

Although they were all badly shaken, everyone reached the island safely. There Davy talked to his men.

Boys, the people of west Tennessee need me to save them and save the country by running for Congress!

I plan to have two laws passed—one to keep fools from going into the wood stave business, and another to hang fake river pilots!

Home again, Davy went hunting. Soon he was able to take a bundle of furs to the store to trade.

How come you have no raccoon skins?

I'm saving them. I plan to run for Congress this fall.

I figure I'll need a couple of fine new caps when I get to Washington!

Sounds like you're sure you're going to win!

Davy did win. He had many friends, and they got people to vote for him.

During his first two years in Congress, Davy stayed quiet and learned. But people soon grew to know him on the streets of Washington.

Who in the world is that?

That's Davy Crockett, the congressman from Tennessee.

Would you tell us about yourself, Congressman?

Why, I'm David Crockett, fresh from the backwoods. I'm half horse, half alligator, and part snapping turtle!

I can wade the Mississippi, leap the Ohio, or ride a streak of lightning. I can also fight wildcats, hug a bear too close for comfort, and make stew out of any man who's against Jackson!

Davy was proud of General Andrew Jackson, who had become president. But in Davy's second term,* he found he didn't always agree with the president.

Gold had been found on Indian land in several southern states. These states now wanted the land for themselves.

That land belonged to the Indians before the white man ever came here! It was given back to the Indians at the end of the Creek war! We must not take it away.

But a bill** was put before Congress that would move the Indians to new lands west of the Mississippi River.

*the two-year period for which a congressman is elected
**an agreement that becomes a law if enough congressmen vote for it and the president signs it

President Jackson wanted the bill to pass. So did all the other Tennessee congressmen. But Davy spoke against it.

It is not fair! I would rather be an old dog belonging to a poor man in the forest than belong to a party that will not be fair to everyone!

Most people did not care about the Indians, and Davy was not sent to Congress that year. But in 1833 he was elected again.

This time he was a leader in the new Whig party.* He was sent to many cities. In Philadelphia they gave him a new, silver-trimmed gun.

Colonel Crockett, the Whig gentlemen of Philadelphia praise you!

In New York . . .

Colonel Crockett, our great city is yours! Here is the key!

And in Boston . . .

Colonel Crockett, our great city is honored . . .

*a political party formed to fight the ideas and plans of Andrew Jackson

But the people at home did not like what Davy was doing.

You voting for Colonel Crockett again?

Not me!

So Davy Crockett did not go back to Washington.

He was angry. He felt the Tennessee people had let him down.

If they don't want me in Tennessee, I'll go to Texas.* Something big's going on down there!

They're fighting to be free from Mexico. They need help!

I wish I could go along, Pa.

Davy left in November, 1835. He reached Texas in January, 1836.

Welcome to Texas, Colonel Crockett!

Greetings to you from the state of Tennessee!

*at this time the land that was to become the state of Texas belonged to Mexico

Later, after a party in his honor, Davy heard some news.

Davy signed the paper.

Men are gathering at San Antonio. We've held the town since December.

I want to help. Will you sign me up to fight in your army?

We're proud to have you! We'll make you a Texas colonel!*

No, no! You don't have to do that.

Davy rode south and west to San Antonio. It was night when he reached the Alamo, an old Spanish mission** used as a fort.

Who are you, stranger?

Davy Crockett of Tennessee— half horse and half alligator!

Jim Bowie, a famous scout, rushed out to welcome Davy.

He's here! Come and meet Davy Crockett of Tennessee!

*a high-ranking officer
**a large church with a wall around it

Colonels Travis and Bowie told Davy how things stood.

Santa Anna, the leader of Mexico's army, is moving toward Texas with his troops.*

He has cannons, too. We have only about 150 men at the Alamo.

But every day we can hold Santa Anna's army here, it's a day longer for the main Texas army to get ready!

Then we had better hold the Alamo!

*When the Mexicans arrived, they surrounded** the Alamo. Santa Anna sent a message: "Give up or die!" Travis answered, "Never!" The battle of the Alamo had begun.*

Make every shot count, men!

Inside the Alamo there was no sleep for anyone. The men ran from one wall to another, as the Mexicans raised ladders.

Quick—to the west wall!

Powder and bullets ran low.

I guess I'll have to start using nails!

Is it as bad as that?

*soldiers
**made a circle around a group or fort so no one could escape

By the end of the battle, men were fighting hand-to-hand. Davy and the other men fought with guns, knives, and fists until not a man among them was still alive.

They had stopped Santa Anna's army for twelve days. The men Santa Anna lost at the Alamo had been his best troops.

Seven weeks later, General Sam Houston and the Texas army defeated the rest of the Mexican army. They had their own battle cry.

Remember the Alamo!

Part of the Alamo still stands in San Antonio today. Davy Crockett was one of the small band of heroes who died there to make Texas free.

Pioneer,* bear hunter, army scout, and "coonskin congressman," Davy Crockett was an American hero even in his own day.

THE END

*one who goes ahead of others to prepare the way for them

Do you remember?

When he went hunting, Davy took along Growler, Deathmaul, Grim, and Holdfast. They were:

a. his guns.   b. his dogs.   c. his horses.

When fighting the Creek Indians, Davy served under a man who would become President. He was:

a. General George Washington.   b. General U.S. Grant.
          c. General Andrew Jackson.

After serving in the army, Davy moved farther west where hunting was poor. To make a living he:

a. built a grist mill.   b. became a farmer.   c. raised cattle.

When Davy Crockett arrived in Washington to serve in Congress, he attracted attention because:

a. he was so tall.   b. he was so famous.

c. he wore a coonskin cap.

Words to know

Can you use these words in sentences of your own?

raiding parties	ford	congressman
scout	ambush	sharpshooters
bill	treaty	Whig party

True or false

1. Davy Crockett was one of eight children.

2. Davy hunted many animals for food, but he was best known for bringing back deer.

3. When Davy joined the Texas army, he was given the rank of captain.

4. Davy often said that he was half horse and half alligator.

5. Davy agreed with the peace treaty which the white men had made with the Indians after the Tallapoosa River Battle.

Questions to think about and discuss

1. In what ways was life in Tennessee hard during Davy's time?

2. Most people have only one or two kinds of jobs during their adult lives. Make a list of the many things Davy did for himself and his country. Why do you suppose there were so many?

3. Like many men of his time, Davy had to fight the Indians. But how did he feel about them personally? How do you know?

4. Why were the people of Texas fighting the Mexicans? How did Davy Crockett happen to become part of that war?

5. All of the Americans fighting at the Alamo were killed. Why, then, is that battle often thought of as a victory for the United States?

Daniel Boone

Written by
NAUNERLE C. FARR

Illustrated by
NESTOR REDONDO

a
VINCENT FAGO
production

Contents

DANIEL BOONE

Daniel Boone lived all his life in Indian country. Once, when there were Indians all around him, he escaped by jumping from a cliff.

Daniel was caught by the Indians many times. He also escaped many times. He was able to stay alive because he knew the ways of the woods.

Then they plowed the ground and planted a crop.

Father Boone also taught his sons everything he knew about the woods.

You must learn to see everything in the woods and to hear every sound.

Most Indians around here are peaceful. But in case a brave* is on the warpath,** you must see him first, and slip away like a shadow!

And you must walk softly so that you don't make any noise.

*a young Indian man
**at war

It is your job to bring the cows home at night. You must notice the sun or the moon, the way the wind blows,—everything. Then you can find your way home again.

These lessons were fun. But they were also a matter of life and death. Daniel learned them well.

As soon as he could hold a gun, Daniel was taught to shoot.

Steady . . . line up your sights.*

Then he learned to hunt.

You got him!

Never waste a shot, Daniel. There's plenty of game,** but you must be careful not to run out of gunpowder.

Daniel loved being in the woods. He soon knew more about them than anyone else.

*the small opening mounted on top of a gun through which one looks to take aim
**wild animals hunted for food

Sometimes he hunted and camped with friendly Indian boys.

You come see Indian village?

I'd like that!

Women do camp work. Indian braves track animals, hunt, fish, fight!

I wish I were an Indian! I think I'd make a good one.

Daniel also listened to the white men tell about Indian fights and Indian tricks they had seen.

There's one thing for sure—you can't trust an Indian. They don't think the way we do!

Daniel kept quiet, but he did not agree.

I *can* think like an Indian. Except for my color, I'm more like an Indian than a white boy!

When Daniel was fifteen, his father decided to move to a new place.

Get ready—we're moving on! This farm land is worn out, and there are too many people coming in.

Where are we going?

Southwest, where there's rich land for sale and lots of game to hunt.

More game, new country to explore,* and fewer people! That's great!

So the Boone family packed up their wagon and began their long journey. They stopped at last in the Yadkin valley in North Carolina.

Plenty of good land, and plenty of grass for the cows.

Someday I'll see what lies west, over the mountains.

Once again they had the hard job of clearing land and building a cabin.**

Somebody has to get us meat, and you're worth any two of us as a hunter! Go ahead, Daniel!

Sure!

*search through
**a small house, often made of logs

Daniel brought back rabbits and turkeys.

Often he shot a deer . . .

. . . and sometimes even a bear.

The skin will make a fine, warm cover!

Daniel became a man. Other families moved nearby. Among them were the Bryans.

Daniel, this is our new neighbor, Rebecca Bryan.

Soon there was a wedding.

Do you, Daniel, take this woman, Rebecca. . . .

The neighbors came from many miles around to join the wedding party.

Daniel and Rebecca built a home. Daniel farmed and hunted. They started a family.

What's behind the mountains, Daniel?

Few men had ever crossed the Allegheny Mountains. * Very little was known about Kentucky, the land beyond.

Nobody knows. Someday I'll find out!

Sometimes friendly Indians came over the mountains.

What's it like on the other side of the mountains?

Great land—big forests. No Indians live there—only hunt and make war there!

Then one day a hunter arrived. His name was John Finley.

Yes, I've been to Kentucky and lived to tell of it. There are bears, deer, buffalo, everything a hunter dreams of!

But the Indians don't want us in Kentucky! And once a man crosses those mountains, he's on his own.

Someday I'm going there!

*a large mountain range that reaches from Pennsylvania to West Virginia

In 1769 Boone, Finley, and six strong men went to see the new land.

We'll look it over and see if it's a good place to live.

We'll get along fine here. The boys are old enough to help with the work.

When the men left, they expected good weather. Instead, it rained for many days.

At night they slept in a lean-to, a kind of tent. The lean-to kept them warm and dry, and hid their fire from the Indians.

Seven weeks later they made their way up the last steep hill to Cumberland Gap. *

There it is, Daniel— Kentucky!

It's beautiful, John, just as you said.

They hurried down to take a closer look at it.

I've never seen so many wild turkeys in my life!

There were great herds of deer.

There were almost as many bears.

They were surprised most of all by the large number of buffalo.

There must be more buffalo here than cattle back home!

*a high place or "pass" that leads from one side of Kentucky's Cumberland Mountains to the other

The men built a small cabin on a river. Then, they went to look around and to hunt.

There's game and rich land everywhere. But it takes other things to make a good place for a settlement.*

You need high ground and a forest that isn't too thick . . . maple trees nearby . . . salt licks** . . . and good water.

They had seen no Indians. Then, on December 22, Daniel was hunting with John Stuart. Suddenly, they found Indians on all sides.

Don't let them know you're afraid. It's the best way.

The Indians took Boone and Stuart with them.

Let them think we're glad to go with them, and that we want to join their tribe.

But don't ever try to escape and *fail*! Then they'll kill you for sure!

*a new town
**a place where rock salt can be found for the animals to lick

By the seventh night, the Indians trusted Boone and Stuart. They even stopped guarding them.

Let's go now!

They moved almost without breathing. One cracking twig would bring certain death!

An Indian moved. They stood very still.

But they got away and even saved their guns. Then they hurried back toward their own camp.

We have a good head start. I don't think they'll chase us.

But when they got back . . .

All our furs have been stolen!

And our friends are gone!

They never heard of their friends again. No one ever knew what had happened to them.

Should we give up and go home?

Not me! I borrowed money to make this trip. I won't go home with nothing to show for it!

We're low on ammunition.*

We don't need our guns. We'll trap beaver and other animals.

So they built another hut, smaller and better hidden, and went to work. One day in January, Daniel saw two men in the woods.

Hello, strangers! Who are you?

We are friends! Don't shoot!

*gunpowder and bullets

It was Daniel's younger brother Squire and a friend. They had come 500 miles to find Daniel.

Well, we've caught up with you at last. We have fresh supplies* and ammunition for you.

Thanks! You're just in time!

Soon the men began hunting again. One night Stuart did not return. The next day, Daniel searched the forest for him.

I found no sign of Stuart!

Let's get away from here! The Indians will find us if we stay!

We can't quit now. This is our chance to be rich.

We'll be very careful!

Stay if you like! I'm going home!

So Neeley left for home—and was never seen again. The Boones hunted and trapped, and did their best to stay away from the Indians. In the spring they had many furs.

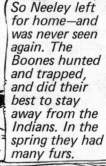

They decided that Squire would go home, sell the furs, and return with more bullets and supplies.

I figure I can be back in two months. Take care of yourself!

You take care! My rifle and I will get along fine!

While he was alone, Daniel saw most of Kentucky. What he learned in his travels would be very useful later.

*things such as food and clothing that people need to live

Squire came back in July. He had sold the furs, paid the money they owed, and bought supplies.

He and Daniel did more hunting and trapping and then went home.

It's hard to believe that these are the little fellows I left behind!

You've been gone a good while, Daniel!

Two years later, Daniel decided to move to Kentucky. Six other families went with the Boones.

It's a good, strong group. We have everything we need to settle in Kentucky.

The trip was a rough and slow one, but at last they camped near Cumberland Gap.

We'll wait here for the forty men who are coming to join us with Captain Russell.

James, you ride back to Russell's cabin and help bring the supplies he promised.

Yes, Father!

On the way back from Russell's cabin, James Boone and his men camped overnight. An Indian war party surprised them at daybreak.

All were killed except two of Russell's men.

The Boones and their friends were sad. Many were frightened.

It's a warning! The Indians want no settlements in Kentucky!

How can forty of us fight thousands of Indians?

We're going back!

Maybe this is not the time. But I'll build a place near here and wait.

The Boones and a few other families decided to stay in a nearby valley.

But Daniel was not there long. Lord Dunmore, the British governor* of Virginia, sent for them.

I have sent men into Kentucky to see the land. But the Indians have attacked them all.

You are the only one who might reach my men and lead them to safety.

I'll go at once!

He had to walk 800 miles in two months. But Daniel led the men out.

*someone who rules a state or a colony; at that time America still belonged to England

Meanwhile, many Indians were making war on the people of Virginia. Finally, however, they were defeated by Dunmore's army.

This gave ideas to a man named Henderson.

Only the Cherokees* still want Kentucky. I'll buy it, then sell it to white men. I'll give you 3,000 acres to help me.

I'll get the Cherokees together for a meeting.

Fine! Then take thirty men and cut a road over the mountains.

The Indians agreed to sell Kentucky to Henderson. Daniel began clearing a road across Cumberland Gap.

Knowing the country, Daniel found a good place for his road. People would come to know it as the Wilderness Road. *In ten weeks he reached the spot he had chosen for their town.*

This is the Kentucky River! I'll send word to Henderson to bring his people here.

Later, the town was named Boonesborough *in Daniel's honor.*

*a group of Indians living in what is now Tennessee and North Carolina

As soon as they arrived, the men began building a fort.

Other men cleared the land and planted crops.

Everyone was pleased when Henderson arrived with forty more men. They knew no one could make them leave now.

Hurrah!

It's my birthday, Daniel! What a party!

Other towns and forts were built nearby. And there was important news.

In Massachusetts they've begun the fight to free us from England's rule!

Soon afterward, Daniel talked to his friend, Richard Callaway.

This place seems strong now. I'm going back to get my family.

I'll go with you and bring *my* family, too.

Daniel returned to Boones-borough in September with Rebecca and Jemima, one of his daughters.

This is the Kentucky River. You are the first white women to see it!

It's beautiful, Daniel!

Nearly a year passed. The Boones were happy. Then one summer day, Jemima and two friends went for a canoe ride. The boat struck some sand and stopped.

We're stuck! Push us off!

I don't want to get my feet wet!

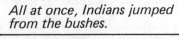

All at once, Indians jumped from the bushes.

No! Stop!

Let us go!

But the Indians grabbed the girls and took them away.

You go with us— and be quiet!

All right.

At sunset the girls were missed. Daniel found their empty canoe.

Indians! They'll head north. We'll follow them.

A broken twig! A scrap of cloth! The girls have tried to leave signs for us!

The men hurried on. Daniel took short-cuts. They went forty miles.

There they are! But be careful! When we sur-prise them, they will try to kill the girls!

Daniel told the men where to shoot. They crept forward without a sound and took aim.

Ready . . . fire!

It's Father!

The Indians who were not killed ran away. The men took the happy girls back home.

Soon the first wedding in Kentucky took place. Betsy Callaway married one of the young men who had saved her from the Indians.

Before long, Jemima Boone and Frances Callaway also married two young men from Boonesborough.

But Indian trouble was getting worse.

The Shawnees* attacked our forts!

The British are giving them weapons to drive us out of Kentucky!

Many frightened families moved back east again.

Only twenty-two guns left to defend Boonesborough!

And not more than a hundred in all of Kentucky!

There was not much food left. And there was no salt to keep meat from spoiling. So Daniel led a party of men to find salt.

They had to boil hundreds of gallons of salt water to get salt. And there was another problem.

We're out of meat, Daniel.

I'll go hunting.

*a group or tribe of Indians who lived in most states east of the Mississippi River

While he was hunting, Daniel was caught by Indians.

There was no chance of escape. Daniel was taken to the Indian chief, Blackfoot.

There are too many of them!

I am happy to see my old friend, the great Chief Blackfoot.

And I, to greet the great white chief, Boone! Welcome!

Blackfoot had many men with him. They were on their way to Boonesborough. And Boonesborough was very weak! Daniel knew he must think of a way to save the fort.

We are tired of fighting. At the right time, we will gladly leave our town.

Don't go now. They are too strong for your small war party!

Wait until spring! Then my people will be happy to move north with you.

So instead of attacking the fort, the Indians went back north to their villages, taking Daniel with them.

Boone, I will make you my son!

You do me a great honor.

Daniel was given the Indian name of Big Turtle.

But still he found no chances to escape. And in the spring a big war party made ready to go to Boonesborough.

Five hundred Indians to attack Boonesborough! I must escape and give some warning!

Later, when he was out hunting, Daniel ran away. The fastest and best Indians chased him. He ran 125 miles in five days to reach the fort.

Daniel! You're safe!

Send some men for help! Make the walls stronger! Bring in plenty of food and water! Indians are coming to attack us!

Soon the Indians appeared.

We have thirty men. Blackfoot has nearly five hundred. We must hold them off as long as we can and wait for help.

For days Daniel kept the Indians away, talking with Blackfoot. But at last the talking ended.

Here they come! We'll defend the fort as long as there is a man left alive!

From behind every tree and bush the Indians fired at the fort.

The women and children made bullets and loaded guns.

Make every shot count, men!

The battle went on for eight days. There was no time to rest. Water ran low, and no help came.

Then the Indians shot blazing arrows onto the dry roofs. They also built fires near the walls of the fort.

Finally, there was no more water.

But suddenly came a clap of thunder, and rain poured down, putting out the fires.

It's a miracle!*

The next morning the Indians were gone. The fort was saved. There would be more battles with the Indians, but from that day on, white people were in Kentucky to stay.

*a strange and wonderful happening, often thought to come from God

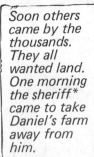

Soon others came by the thousands. They all wanted land. One morning the sheriff* came to take Daniel's farm away from him.

I'm sorry, Daniel! But some people say you don't own your farm.

I've opened up miles and miles of land to these people and fought off Indians. Now they want to take away my small part of it?

So Daniel lost his farm. It was not until many years later that the United States government voted to give him 1,000 acres.

There are too many people and towns here! It's time we moved along.

They went west to Missouri. At that time it belonged to Spain, and people knew all about Daniel Boone there.

Señor** Boone, it is an honor to have you here! We will give you 1,000 acres of land.

He accepted their offer gladly.

Daniel Boone lived to be eighty-six years old. People never stopped coming to visit him to hear his stories.

Tell us one of your Indian stories, Mr. Boone!

I will. But first I'll tell you about the lands to the west. There are so many places still left to explore!

THE END

*a person who sees that the laws of a small town are kept
**the Spanish word for "Mr."

Do you remember?

When he was three years old, Daniel Boone's father moved to a settlement that became:

a. New York.   b. Vermont.   c. Pennsylvania.

Daniel Boone explored the land and cut a trail to Cumberland Gap, opening up the area that became:

a. Ohio.   b. Kentucky.   c. Kansas.

Daniel was taken into an Indian tribe as Chief Blackfoot's son. He was given the name of:

a. Flying Dove.   b. Big Turtle.   c. Hunting Owl.

Daniel warned the settlers that 500 Indian braves would attack:

a. Boonesborough.   b. New York.   c. Santa Fe.

Words to know

Can you use these words in sentences of your own?

Cumberland Gap   governor   ammunition
supplies   miracle   game
settlement   sheriff   explore

True or false

1. Daniel Boone grew up in the eastern part of the United States. But when he moved west, he went to Oklahoma.

2. Daniel made money by trapping wild animals and selling them to zoos.

3. A man named Henderson promised Daniel 3,000 acres of land if he would help buy it from the Indians and build a road to the new town.

4. Early settlements needed forts to protect them from Indians and wild animals.

5. Daniel got along well with the Indians, even though at different times he had to fight them.

Questions to think about and discuss

1. Why did the sheriff of Boonesborough take Daniel's land away from him? Do you think this was fair to Daniel? If the sheriff had let Daniel keep his land, would it have been fair to the other settlers?

2. At the bottom of page 41 is a picture of Daniel's wedding reception. In what ways is it different from those we attend today? How is it the same?

3. Why was it important for Daniel to understand the Indians and how they lived?

4. Make a list of things that had to be done in order to start a new settlement in Daniel's time.

5. How many times did Daniel risk his own life to save or help his friends? Do you think he was a hero? Why or why not?